CHAPPED LIPS
POEMS

LANCEE WHETMAN

Copyright © 2025 Lancee Whetman

Visit the author's website at www.vigilancee.org

All rights reserved. No part of this publication may be reproduced, distributed, or transmitted in any form or by any means, including photocopying, recording, or other electronic or mechanical methods, without the prior written permission of the publisher or author, except in the case of brief quotations embodied in critical reviews and certain other noncommercial uses permitted by copyright law.

Names, characters, events, and incidents are the products of the author's imagination. Any resemblance to actual persons, living or dead, or actual events is purely coincidental.

ISBN: 979-8-9897302-1-6

*I'm acknowledging the feeling
that I'd rather be where you are
more than anywhere else right now.*

*Obvious, but aloud,
I miss you.*

C.L.

XOXO
to the one that got away
(turns out it was me)

to men
women
mended hearts
&
hearts on the mend

POEMS

chapped lips 1
cloudy with a chance of ChapStick 2
coffee table rings 4
i wish i was 5
Twin Lakes trek 6
to the stranger on the street 8
one hundred and one thefts 9
fog clearing 10
urban lover 11
homerun 12
simple phenomenon 13
your eyes tell stories 14
combing the beach 16
lunchbox note 17
unzip 19
second-date sam 20
squall 24
responding to a personal in the New York Times Book Review Magazine 25
shhhh 27
novice fisherwoman 28
Minnesotan man 33
spring's invitation to melt 34

conibear	36
swim	37
what is your (spicy) love language?	42
fishing	43
tiny beautiful things	44
easter sunday	45
mashup	46
epigraph of a body	47
when you say nothing at all	49
folding my laundry	51
clear skies Cody	53
sp(ring) cleaning	56
all you need is a light jacket	58
leave our initials	59
calendula on metal	61
pH 3	62
cannibalism	63
the help of nelly	64
dating-app dilemma	65
dating exercise	66
T-Pain started covering my favorite songs	67
hi, Miss-demeanor	68
western nights	69
True Grit	70
interject	72
glow in the dark	73

pool boy	74
tundra vixen	75
puzzle	76
laguna arson	77
Cinderella reimagined	78
woman in S.T.E.M.	79
snap him no filter	80
to-do list	82
outdated Denny's	83
if the world was ending	85
earthquake	86
leap year	87
duration unknown	90
confectionary concoc[k]tions	91
insertion	92
stolen love	93
what's brewing?	94
how ergonomic are soulmates?	95
elysian end	96
Cumberland Gap	97
pleated skirt	98
sour(dough)	99
pole dancer	100
the street I grew up on as my porn star name	103
little miss pissed off	104
Bar None	106

sisyphus	108
sunset coffee shop	109
kings of homecoming	110
Luddite lover	111
i wish you were here	113
thirst	114
be good, Charlotte	115
whistleblower voice	118
mayonnaise	120
mighty convincing	121
red herring	122
antidote	123
nothing personal, just never want to see you again	125
coming-down comeuppance	127
jest	128
pyrotechnics	129
i've seen it all before	130
right-of-way	131
til' death (or divorce) do us part	132
007	135
making up	136
stinging nettle	137
friction	138
pilots	139
been bitten before	140
tiny encounters with restraint	141

don't forget me..142
splinter..143
women my age are...144
pretty like poetry...145
at the club..146
holding too tightly..147
limbo...148
this poem has already been written, but....................149
exile..150
boy with the blues..151
About the Author...152
Acknowledgments 153

LANCEE WHETMAN

CHAPPED LIPS

checkered sheet, checkmate
conspicuous cherry-red cheeks.
an old-fashioned suitor
suits me well, I find
what being found
feels like.
honey,
these once-chapped lips
have met
a nice
chap.

pucker up.

LANCEE WHETMAN

CLOUDY WITH A CHANCE OF CHAPSTICK

paperclip tendencies
loosely held by cactus
relationships.

flimsy invitations
unresponded-to texts &
save-for-later sexts.

will respond now
(or never).

electronic swipe.
go left or right
to get to hell.
fire-starter match.

complicated 100-word biographies.
comfortable silence.

interest rate is zero.
sign up now
for hedonistic headboards!

dine-in blunders.
dine-out blunders.
more of the same
stir-fry pansexuality.

CHAPPED LIPS

oceanic breakups.
I'm an endangered
pucker fish.

captain heartbreak.
first mate lust.
lost court*ship*.

sane is the weather.
Cloudy with a chance of ChapStick.

COFFEE TABLE RINGS

Weaving yearning into the
threads of my vocabulary.
Longing from afar
tucked sheepishly behind
yesterday's outdated headlines.
The only rings here
are on the coffee table
as my left fingers have
unfettered fret
nervously flipping newsprint
textualizing what I want
(to use the pronoun *us*)
and Wordle my way into your next
nonfiction selection—
this feeling must be factual.
Check you out
bookmarked for eternity.
I am a rainy-day read
abruptly detaining an *I love you*
in my larynx
for now.
But as the writer
of this
I know one day
it'll surely be
the last line.

I WISH I WAS

5:13 p.m.
Walking into the strip-mall
Vietnamese restaurant
for our first date.
*Insignificant or
telling of a larger narrative?*
I wish I was:
a darling Dahlia
a Celtic cross
a taking-of-turns
sharing our stories.
We are but another cleaned plate
after a filling meal.
Phở stomachs full of laughter,
digesting a future *sorry*.
That napkin-pressed night
ushered in
the opening of doors
the changing of thermostats
and the switching over
of each other's laundry.
Without reservations,
just like that first date,
I jump, as he does,
into the smoke
and mirrors
that reflect
what we could have been.

TWIN LAKES TREK

a quarrel at the quarry,
there's no

space

to pull off to the side
to park the truck
for a thrill-seeking ski.

an up-hiller and down-hiller personality
decide to peruse the woods
flatly in the fog.

a plan departed for a new one
imprinting a tender track
in the snow.

by chance, they witness a canvas
of spruce dancers lining the
river in quiet jubilance,
brush-stroked into
a ballroom full of blue.

a pastel gown glow, twirling
in the humble limelight.

CHAPPED LIPS

the stream and its calm libations
guides them, as they,
from a last-minute invitation,
are whisked away into
dusk's doting dance.

LANCEE WHETMAN

TO THE STRANGER ON THE STREET

*are we making love
or just eye contact?
is there middle ground
in fantasyland?
iris-induced idyllicism
figment of my future
or just a*

drive-by daydream?

something in my throat is
telling me to
speak
in semi-understandable smiles
at a two-second

stop.

I'll reverse the mileage
beneath this
tired rubber

just to relive it all over
and

    pour

        out

            gallons

                of myself

to someone

    I'll never actually

             meet.

CHAPPED LIPS

ONE HUNDRED AND ONE THEFTS

the start to my day / and the end to it, too / the left side of the bed / my ring finger / a last name / my every day of the week / my mind's long-term storage / my copilot seat / the steam from the kettle, piping hot / the second space in the toothbrush holder / the top shelf in the color-coordinated closet / my mom's approval / a key to my apartment / my heart.

FOG CLEARING

Linen dress is summer's exile.
Asking the stream about ethics

but it only knows orchestra.
I get a dose of a wet kiss,

sun fuel, slight breeze.
Open-pasture body.

Minimize the distance between
belts. I want Spanish sunsets

the lifting of la niebla
& Pablo Neruda poems

smeared all over
the sky.

URBAN LOVER

The highline is ignited. Illumination of LED pollution, lights, and limousines. Car cacophony causes cement to harden more. Stuck between bumper-to-bumper (cymbals). These red-light pauses are exhausting. Wearing my high-top sneakers down tired infrastructure, a concourse of street signs. Always at the behest of a flashing blinker. The cobbling concrete caves in with the weight of foot commutes. Passersby, each with an ear bud of noise but nothing to say to each other. Close contact, still no closure or communication that's authentic. We're strangers walking along. Above the city is the sky that we cannot see, and haven't for weeks, and may never with all of this "progress" obstructing the cosmos. The only hope here is in the hands of someone handsome. I am fortunate enough to have him to hold in this makeshift heaven. Towering over us, is too many Babels, crumbling with each passing century. For now, I'll capture his carbon exhale—it's the least I can do as an urban lover.

HOMERUN

What becomes of us
you play out a million times in your head.

Don't be frightened to inquire about partnership status or Friday night plans. If she scares you, perhaps you're still just a boy blaming the world for a lack of fish. To pursue a girl is one thing you've mastered, but to pursue a woman is another.

Checkers to chess, respectively.

Only one game demands that the queen be more powerful than the king. If you try to out*man*euver her, such futile attempts will get you nowhere. Walk her to her door, meet the parents. A word to the wise: Play the long game—but don't rest on your laurels. Shoot straight for the heart, even if you stutter.

She's anything but a quick hitter, and bases are loaded. Don't strike out without attempting to swing, backwards K.

Are you out or in? It's up to you.
Steal a base.
Steal a heart.
We're all scared of sliding into (a) home,
but we make the attempt anyway.

What if you score a forever?

CHAPPED LIPS

SIMPLE PHENOMENON

The physics of bicycles and spin tops,
the unsolved mini mysteries of the world.
Oh, how the simplest phenomenon—
like you—
dumbfounds even Einstein.

YOUR EYES TELL STORIES

your eyes
tell stories
of Sagittarius.
put a Pistol Star
in my hip holster
and arch my back
into conspiracy.
the universe won't pull
the arrow out of my
chest where
milky quartz is encircled:
the way I believe
in innocence
still, crystallized
in the heart of the galaxy.

your elemental eyes
tell tales
of 88 constellations.
naming me: *water bearer*
naming you: *flying fish*
and crowning me
in Corona Borealis
making me your majesty
of Mensa.

CHAPPED LIPS

midwinter
twinkling in Taurus
atop this mountain,
your eyes tell
narratives of this
interstellar night—
our particulate dust
dodged daylight
a time or two.

your eyes tell stories of the
Andromeda account:
when you walked past me
on this exact day, last year,
you knew you must say *hello*.
and tonight,
you turn my ring finger
to stone.

LANCEE WHETMAN

COMBING THE BEACH

fishing out pastels
from the horizon.
round earth
sunset theory
beachcombing for freckles
at the intertidal zone.
intersecting hands, clammy
us, searching through silt
for each other.
seashell-encased discoveries—
something of interest
or perhaps
just two people
made of pearl.

LUNCHBOX NOTE

no grand gesture
nothing gargantuan
like break-the-bank bouquets.
he tends to our budding garden
acts articulated by
a lunchbox note:
I wish I was eating you out
and etching ice off of
my truck's windshield
for a prompt work arrival.
it's thermostat adjusting
for the optimal comfort
of cold-blooded body temperatures.
leaving a thrifted book
on my nightstand
that made him think of me—
Advanced Chemistry, First Edition.
quelling anxiety
with a shared location and ETA
I'll be home soon reassurances
holding my hand in between
the switching of gears
in the single-cab baby-blue Ford.
a *you-do-the-cooking* and
I'll-do-the-dishes agreement.
a held-open door, every time.
picking my favorite roadside daisy,
calling me *crazy*,

sharing our lazy
days and nights:
an exhibition of
love, daily.

UNZIP

I tell him it is
better to be alone
than badly accompanied
and he agrees
that we've both been
too cold for too long
and it ain't
getting much warmer
in these parts.
the only level-
headed lovers here, us
pining for pike, oddly enough,
each other, too.
he places his hand on my back,
briefly so, but barely enough
to send a shiver storm
down to T9,
recalling what a touch can do.
without a voice to utter
what we should do next,
in this sprawled-out woodland
next to the river,
he un-muddles the water
and begins unzipping.

LANCEE WHETMAN

SECOND-DATE SAM

ice-skate (date?)
we walk up together
to the warming room
to tie blades to our soles.
our mutual friends Charlie and Tuck
ask me: *did you come here with Sam?*
I stutter an *uh yeah.*

afterwards, we walk to his
apartment at the Salmon Inn,
once a Subway sandwich shop
evidenced by the wallpaper maps
of unidentifiable railway stops
and 2-D brick plastered to the walls—
almost makes the space feel
like a cozy Italian eatery
in this town of 2,000.

he invites Tuck and Charlie
over for a drink with us, too.
Charlie: boxed wine.
Tuck: a beer.
Sam is unphased
telling them I am staying
for dinner, with him,
after their departure.
Sam pours me a
glass of peaty whiskey
sharpens my dull knives

CHAPPED LIPS

for approximately half an hour
calling it *meditation*
as we both reveal our
dating nonconformities
be it: *fluid* preferences.
he feels safe.
he's a liberal.

he touches me only once
the whole evening.
a gentle and playful
forearm gracing
as I derail us
on another conversational
tangent.
neurodivergence.

he speaks of the Marshall Islands—
his second audiology job
remotely administering
ABR (auditory brainstem response) tests.
he is current
on the events
of the country's GDP—
how it is mostly comprised
of U.S. fund inflow
for the time it
nuclear tested in Oceania.
Sam aspires for diplomat status
reads *The Economist*,
for "fun."

Sam showcases his culinary enthusiasm
with mapo tofu
and cast-iron chocolate chip cookies—
under-baked and doughy
(just how I like)—
to satiate my sweet tooth
all while doing the
chef-style
dish-towel-over-the-shoulder bit
(oh so naturally).

while I do the dishes,
I thank my stepdad for
teaching me the immediacy
of drying just-washed knives
as I hand Sam
(and his inseparable dishtowel)
the cleaver
directly from my sudsy hands.

Sam insists I borrow his free-store
fantasy fiction novel, *Wintersmith*
by Terry Pratchett.
optimistically, he believes I'll like it.
skeptically, I believe I won't.
(in hindsight, I do).
it's whimsical, accentuated in
Scottish brogue dialogue.

CHAPPED LIPS

he grants me
the honor of annotation
to engage with the text
as if it were my own—
my language of *woo-ing*.
from his collected mound of
Discworld discoveries
he lends me this new genre
to explore
this dalliance.

like any book, or lover,
I always (initially)
begin to wonder
how they all will
eventually end.
I set this thought aside as
we read, out loud,
to each other, the first lines.
to see which book
has the best introduction,
saving ourselves
from any
spoiler alerts
and even
finality.

SQUALL

Remember late May and the on-and-off-again squalls? When it was too wet for summer but too bronze for spring? Finally,

the pouring subsided, and we sequestered ourselves to the tundra. With the XTRATUF-high bog water nearing the brim of our boots,

trudging, we went, as the tide barged out to the Nushagak Bay. To our dismay, we safely stayed in the dry-sock zone. It was

glorious mud that covered our clothes, a slip-and-slide through silt, so silly, our clumsy hearts. I thought of nothing but you, Cody,

the coast, and the clay on Howdy's fur—the remnants of the Wood River that I'd have to wash off of her later. You offered up

your dog-washing services and a willingness to get wet with, or shall I say, alongside, me—lathering up our laugher for the

long haul. Apparently, you enjoyed the spectacle of my long legs from behind, you told me, as you, and your gun, got ready to

go home. Kissing my lips before you left, it finally started to rain, tears of joy touched delicate earth.

CHAPPED LIPS

RESPONDING TO A PERSONAL IN THE NEW YORK TIMES BOOK REVIEW MAGAZINE

Washington, D.C., 29 M, lawyer, 6'5", lean, no/latent/patent defects, seeks free-thinking woman who doesn't want kids. iamexactlyasdescribed@gmail.com

---

2/29/2023
2:49:00 p.m.

Hi undisclosed name,

I am a 27-year-old female. 6'0". Just-budding lawyer, transitioning out of the profession for poetry. Fairly freethinking. Unknown on kids, certain on dogs.

I have never read the *New York Times Book Review* magazine before, but call it serendipity or what have you, I decided to read something new in the literary department today and stumbled upon this personal by pure accident—flipping to the end of the magazine while trying to determine how long a book-review magazine actually is since I've never read one before.

Upon my stumble, I outright cackled from this posting. Did you create this for content or actual solicitations? Either way, it's perfect. I'm clickbait.

Sending this email into a void alternative time zone. Disclaimer: I'm in Alaska. (Should such geographical disclaimers be at the beginning or end of an introduction? Not sure of the rules of engagement here).

Always beautiful tomorrows,

Lancee
The Rosy-Cheeked Poetess

CHAPPED LIPS

SHHHH

Have you ever hit replay
on a whisper? Rewound

silence? It is a hush's way
of hissing at us. Close

the outlet of our mouths.
I am desperate to extricate

an *I love you*. I am desperate
to hear anything. Anything

from you,
at all.

NOVICE FISHERWOMAN

it's small-town talk
when I go and sit
down next to you.
let them speculate
spectate
at this basketball game
something other than
what's happening on
the hardwood as we
hold each other's gaze into
the fourth quarter.

us, bleacher-bound
catching up
in a different
setting beside our Friday night
jam sessions and piano lessons.
you ask
(after I've disclaimed I am a
novice snow-machine rider
and even more of a
novice fisherwoman):
do you want to come along
on a snowgo ride?
I've got an extra.
I am going to spear pike.

CHAPPED LIPS

I say, without hesitation: *yes*.

an hour later, I'm outfitted
in every layer I own
throttling the tundra
trailing him and his
sled of ice-fishing gear—
we're to try out his
new Finnish hand auger
for the first time.

we're on the west side
of Warehouse Mountain
slithering our way up
Snake river.
He knows each open
stream crossing, keeps
an eye out for otter and
beaver tracks, for trapping.
he checks in with me
and my chilled hands.

once he selects the scenic site
in the vastness of this place
I am sent on a mission
to cut five to six alder branches.
in a silent showcase,
with clear direction
he demonstrates how to use
his hand saw.
the branches are to be used
to mark the drilled holes upon
a future return.
the auger quickly penetrates
through two feet of ice,
with a natural piercing effort,
he does the same to me.

We jig for lethargic pike
pondering if we like
each other in a
more-than-friendly way.

I disclose my love for poetry
and apparently his
mother, whom he speaks
highly of (good sign),
writes, too. I begin reeling up
more feeling
than fish.

CHAPPED LIPS

how communicative
is a glance?
I notice his eyes are brown
when I share my packed
snacks of freeze-dried ice cream
and dark-chocolate macadamia nuts.

he catches an
arctic char within minutes.
showcases it to me while down
on one knee.
my best friend says: *it's basically*
a bush Alaska proposal.

the culmination of the trip,
however,
ends hours later
in his fisherman's loft,
well-maintained, just like
his machines.
he plays the *next time*
card, that if I bring s'mores
he'll light the fire for us
on our forthcoming adventure.

the two of us had rung in 2024
together, as friends,
earlier that year.
then, I was
on a tail end of a tailspin.
unsure what lay below
winter's temporal ice.

now,
I am finally learning
how to fish
for the right species
of man.

CHAPPED LIPS

MINNESOTAN MAN

Tiger Balm my shoulders. Chiropractor my back. Tell me to relax. Gentle realignment. Thumb through knots. Rye bread. Carbohydrate kneads (needs). Loaf through family histories. Doughy time. Kitchen closeness. Square-foot bodies. My recipient eyes catch a brown-eyed wink midair. High heating bills. Forage a 52-card deck. Word through Funk and Wagnalls. How does a Midwesterner say *roof*? Say it a million times more. Sounds gruff. Peppered scruff. Accounting for age. Relocating closer, to me. Cattle ranch my chest. Heart opener. Unabridged tension. *Walking in Memphis*, call me *ma'am*. His mama raised a good one. Tell me what's yours is mine, *let's share a rural life*? Hometown temptation, say *come visit. Do we really feel the way we feel?* Tooth-extraction cute. No-Novocain night. Double-dip permission. Podcast laughs. Let's do an instrumental poetry segment on the radio—hard launch, call it *going public*. Piano man, sharp wit. Left-hand accompaniment. Make me treble, clef. We're lyrics-in-the-making. Utensils face up, dishwasher logic. *Let's do this again, soon.* Staying late stuck between my teeth. Yearning floss. Dental goodnight. April is calving (cuffing) season.

LANCEE WHETMAN

SPRING'S INVITATION TO MELT

Vertical aspirations,
chasing March
(again)
and the changing of the seasons.
Bedding
down
into someone familiar.

Forest exploration:
a hand-built cabin
with a surplus of nails
driven towards inhabiting
a finished pined product.
Wood-stove ambiance.
Vulnerability flames.
White glitter on the ground outside—
spring's invitation to melt.
That's the power that powder can have
in the land of magic carpet rides.
One more pull of gravity:
Turn left to go right—
I don't understand
the physical logic quite yet,
but *leaning*
into your seniority
feels stable to me.

CHAPPED LIPS

Wool cloth finds rest on milled floors,
where it belongs,
off of us.
Hands attach themselves
to a willing
counterpart.
Let our neuroticisms get the best of us
as we take vertebrae chances.
Crevasse release,
subdued relaxation,
firm sleep.

I break all that you have fixed,
but in doing so,
you forgive in gentle
equanimity.
Your presence
has the tendency to mend
more and more
of me
without even
knowing it.

CONIBEAR

cuddle-me-up like a conibear
in the corner of the cabin
firm grasp, no trap
just morning kinesiology.
hush of hands in quiet
interlocking. *rush!*
make me blush
under quilted starlight.
jig-and-saw days
a woods-and-water duo.
get me unstuck
it's a heat problem,
you determine,
matter-of-factly,
and I feel it:
the mechanics of a wink
melting into a mountainside view.
hold me bowline-tight,
Dyneema-tethered.
Lynx Lancee, I'm a cat-
ch. monitor my every movement
snow angel stars above Aleknagik.
here's the thing:
while all I want to do is wander
I find myself liking
very much, wandering away
in this place, wildly
with you.

CHAPPED LIPS

SWIM

*The first day of summer is the last
day of summer*, an Alaska adage.

It's 81 degrees here—
the equivalent to 115 degrees
in the lower forty-eight.
Which means we take a long
weekend.
Which means we take
lake days
expending our sick leave
for the sun.
For once,
the heat becomes
more enemy
than depression.

That late July,
he invited me
to his hand-built cabin
which took him seven years
to complete.
I've been sad for fourteen.
Incomplete still.

He proudly
shows me pictures
of the building process.
Stubborn nails.

Wet pine.
Sweat. Sawdust.
He recounts
10-foot walls
toppling down
then resurrecting.
The foundation.
The stabilization.
The finalization.

I, too, know what it is like
to labor,
albeit internally.

He launches the boat
to get to that spruced place
lined with irises
now
salmonberries ripening
huckleberries forthcoming.

The lake:
glassy smooth.
My mind
craving solace,
solitude.

Searching.

CHAPPED LIPS

I want coursing veins.
I want a clear mind
calm thoughts.
I want Cody,
but I need myself
more.

The mountains surrounding us
are more metaphor than scenery.
I know they are unconquerable
through the alders.
I gaze at them
unmoored from myself.
Acclimatizing to sea legs.

Sow and cubs bobbing
for fish nearby.
Mere mergansers
flapping overhead.

I ask him to stop
in the middle
of the lake
so I can get
into the cool
blue water.

I tell him:
Hydrotherapy.

I mean:
A reminder
A reprieve.

A relapse of life.

I strip down
to the bare necessities—
zinc-oxide body.

My toes
confront the bow's ledge,
asking for bravery.

Here, leaps of
faith
are not hardened.
There is no wake
today.
No shallows
to get stuck in.

He says:
Here's a lifevest.

I reject it
and jump.

How do you tell
someone you love
that this is the only time
you ever feel

CHAPPED LIPS

weightless?

WHAT IS YOUR (SPICY) LOVE LANGUAGE?

My love language is touched by Tabasco, cuddled by Cholula. It's a habanero wink. RedHot, frankly. It's lovers in Louisiana. Cayenne bayou. It's New Mexico Hatch chiles. Christmas year round. A vinegar twinkle. My love languages are green and red. My love language is bell-pepper mad. It's sriracha sheets. Sweat-inducing smiles. It's scorpion. It's diablo. It's Mad Dog. It's mild, medium, hot, extra spicy. My love language is the devil's appetite.

CHAPPED LIPS

FISHING

hold me
caudal-peduncle style
to the fin-
ish.

release.

LANCEE WHETMAN

TINY BEAUTIFUL THINGS

Tiny beautiful things
are all around me.
Champagne surprises
and roadside daisies
are antidotes;
antidepressants.

He says:
We're celebrating life today.
And I know that
he makes me
still want to.

CHAPPED LIPS

EASTER SUNDAY

postpone Easter
family calls
food-pyramid precedents.
halve the pie
leftover belly.
stain the eggs
huckleberry violet:
the purpler the better.
moose-bone distractions
for my rowdy puppy. *Howdy!*
yearn for fresh air
walk a new route
plan our next holiday
together.
put "popcorn" in the
bucket—
list all the things
I want to do
with
to
and
for
you.

LANCEE WHETMAN

MASHUP

Is it problematic that I think
Jay-Z's voice is nostalgic?

This excitable life all began
back in 1995. Nineties DNA.
Cassette heart thinning into
a CD-ROM: scratched, skips
the good parts, sometimes.
Evolving into a new decade
with a hum-drum of him,
a record-spinning savior.

A rap-tap re-charge of my voice:
a star feature, controlling the
volume, shuffling along
with somebody else's
early-80's soundtrack:
a multimedia connection
R&B banter
a song through the
multi-verse.
infinite realms
of us, on the airwaves,
in our mashup era.

EPIGRAPH OF A BODY

VIP status
enter into my mind
without brain-bouncer restraint.
a backstage pass
to my bedroom.
crown chakra fumes
fantasies of him,
short circuit a neural pathway.
red-stiletto daydream
lion's breath
to body oscillation.
snow-globe romanticism
shaken up
blizzards of purkinje
quiver of a back.
cloth avalanche
on mattress mountain.
headboard climber
call him *trad daddy*
adrenaline steam.
soft surrender.
massaging the mood
with lavender skin—
midnight friction.

dimmed bulbs
kill-switch kiss—
I, take it from behind
just so I don't have to
look at him.
unbound by just-trimmed stubble,
hegemony of my heart.
revealing to him,
my bodily epigraph
before he decides if
I am something worth
reading
over and over
again.

WHEN YOU SAY NOTHING AT ALL

There's this thing about timing: It's a fussy son-of-a-gun. Doesn't like to operate on clockwork's mechanisms—it's always a few minutes early or astoundingly late. But timing knows what to play on the jukebox late on a Friday night. On an evening drooling for something alcoholic. Something banjo-infused. Something that would make a man giddy with the gumption to ask a girl to dance. Timing. The drinks: half-priced. The tunes: all bluegrass. *Ain't it funny how old songs stir up new feelings?*

Within a leather wallet lay a few $1 bills to tip the bartender for the slew of PBRs that ended up on their table that night. Within their eyes laid love. From across the room, inquisitive and needing, were they. In the place where broken-in boots really knew how to dance around a legion of other feet, stepping in pairs of two, encircled by cowboy hats and fringe. Drenched in clandestine neon, in a tipsy orbit, there's a tendency to tether ourselves to spurious spurs—until a true one finally digs into your skin so much you can't ignore the feeling.

Timing. That thing I mentioned earlier, played it so cool like it was smoking a cigarette on a rooftop, overlooking a small-town kingdom, pleased with the happenings all around it. It was right on schedule that night, when he walked over to her table. *Ma'am*, was his introduction. *Howdy*, was hers. Leading the way, he clasped her hands in his in an irreverent country prayer of some sort. And the rest needed no dialogue, as the lyrics provided all the context. Slow sentences were timing's sweet accomplice. The song: *When You Say Nothing At All* by Alison Krauss. Whisked away, two falling into a moment, without warning. Held close, holding near, to one another. They paid no mind to the ticking minute and hour arrows on the wall, clueless as to the bar's impending closure. Yet again, timing knew it had done a mighty fine job—always by surprise or by unexpected serendipity does it effortlessly labor. Timing does its best work when people seem to pay it no damn mind at all.

CHAPPED LIPS

FOLDING MY LAUNDRY

chalk it up to the snowstorm,
make the day
a flurry of facsimile texts.
there's not much
on my shoulders
these days,
yet I still feel the weight
of your absence.
you've got mettle
for mending this mess,
folding my laundry,
offering me your shirt—
on the line, is us
hung up
on forever, and ever.
tethering is quite a powerful fabric—
we're being pulled toward
threaded proximity.
magnets can mystify
and make us
be darned,
sock fools.
what're you wearing?
wool?
keep me warm
then wick away
whetted tears
from this rosacea.

I know that commitment
is a fear—
but you make it feel
velvet-soft
something that'll
last,
something that
won't be
closeted,
something that
my body
will never want to
take off.

CLEAR SKIES CODY

at Lazy L Ranch,
take a nap
while I draw
you near (in my mind).

lacy,
racing crimson
beneath this bone-plated heart.
when you return,
this negligee
will no longer be held
by negligence.

on display are the stars,
where you are.
walk amongst them,
as you tend to the cattle
in your care.

low-grunting harmonies
white-pine prophecies,
collected breath under Andromeda.

look up!
see a shooting star
profess your wish
and risk it
to tell me to be *there*,
next to you,
witnessing the same
clear sky.

Cody,
the universe is
conspiring.
we're just its
willing pawns
fawning
from our inherent feralities.
going wild or wistful—
take your pick.

magic can't be undone
even when you break
the rules of divulging.
the only justification
I can come up with
is that we're made up of
the same elements,
aching to return to alignment
just like our cosmic counterparts.

CHAPPED LIPS

we're thermostat and theory:
a perfect exemplar
that not everything has to have
an explanation that we must
understand.

so I'll let all your future wishes
do to me what they will,
willingly,
god-willing
that you'll return
crashing into me
and this chest cavity
with those brown-eyed meteors
like the Big Bang.

SP(RING) CLEANING

rearrange a room
apartment feng shui.
the couch sits
in a new spot
next to the piano.

he admits he liked it better
when the white-and-black keys
were by the window
so he could
play the delicate chords
and wait
and watch
as I arrived
each evening
at his place.

at least
now
the armchair has
made its exit
the curtains
opened
the neon yellow carpet
is gone
rolled up
and wood
exposed
cleaned floorboards

CHAPPED LIPS

band around the walls.
the room is rich
and earthy again:
a morning espresso
dark and lingering
on your palette.

repotted plants
are placed
on the left-hand side
of the windowsill
for decorative sake.

he gets down
on one knee.
the room is altered
and we are, too.

ALL YOU NEED IS A LIGHT JACKET

morning dew, gingerly rain type-of-weather woman. gentle breeze baby, swish of a skirt—like April 25th. light-jacket vernacular, I read old-English novels—nod in the novelty of your spring stubble stroking against the grain of my cheekbone. inquisitive eyebrow raises. *I dare you to kiss me.* tucked away in cottonwood troves, twisted up like pretzels. we're a prophecy of the present, in the wake of the weekend, sprawled out on a quilt, where we exchange quips: hip-to-hip, lip-to-lip. guardian of the picnic basket, made of interdigitating birch. you are adroit at apple-bobbing and riverside parlance. tacit tenderness, as we touch in this mountain wilderness—a realm where we revel in (and rightly so). to refract a lover's gaze is a rite-of-passage.

CHAPPED LIPS

LEAVE OUR INITIALS

it's 12:08 a.m.
and I feel the weight
of April's absence.
low murmurs of my heart
beckon for warmth.

there's no end to it
perhaps the 29th?
returns are flighty.
it's a plight,
these late-night poems:
desperado songs.

I see the sun
where you are.
it reaches to us both
while we reach
to each other's distances,
longitudes.
I just want latitude to love.

what if we etch our names
on a nearby tree trunk
for romance's sake?
sappy.
leave our initials on South Dakota
or a spruce—
either will suffice.

I want a dirt road
but not the one here.
I'd trade this MUCH
for the Midwest, NOW.
I make demands I can't have.
a soda, *POP*.
Minnesota reprieve,
a carbonated cuddle
I thirst for.

there are plenty of salmon
in Southwest Alaska
scales of spring,
but I'm feeling selFISH lately.
It's a slow dance
high-heeled waiting
aching soles (souls)
as I wander through
our once-shared woods.
impervious to snow
and starry nights.
I'll melt, at dawn.
Y a w n i n g
as this early-morning yearning
seeps out
of
a
tear
duct.

CHAPPED LIPS

CALENDULA ON METAL

dilatory orbs of steel-fleshed eyes:
a freshly oiled blinking.
remote-controlled emote-r
with rechargeable love
clutching calendula bouquets
with titanium-forged hands.
screw-top head
turning you on
turning you 'round
turning you into
an electromagnetic receiver.

in the flamboyance
of ordinary robotics,
a bot bought supermarket flowers
on its own volition.
bionic mannerisms
but no sensory programming
for petal-smelling.
unpracticed
in the mechanics
of doting,
standing before you
displaying full-charge affection—
do your aluminum loins feel the spark yet?

LANCEE WHETMAN

PH 3

Just a girl
who loves
anything acidic:
- kombucha
- pickled onions
- *you.*

CANNIBALISM

There are ten (10) human body parts
that are only three (3) letters long:
eye
hip
arm
leg
ear
toe
jaw
rib
lip
gum.

I chew on
you.

THE HELP OF NELLY

sharpie my number on a crumpled dive-bar napkin // leverage lust with ruby red lips and crop-top cleavage // let the cat eyeliner puuurrrrrowl // go rogue and pose like a Vogue star in your snap story // a first-try bullseye babe // coax you to the dance floor // build hands-to-hips heat with the help of Nelly // back-and-forth banter to the bass // take you back to my place, consensually // phone on do not disturb now // undress one another in head-nod confirmation // it's negative-twenty degrees outside // but damn // it's getting hot in herre

DATING-APP DILEMMA

Swipe right: Spouse or spam?
Bumble, Tinder, Hinge—oh my!
Husband? Wife? I'm bi.

DATING EXERCISE

Trying to get my ass, fit.
His profile says he's
very active.
see you later sedentary-ism!
boxing with these matches
fitness, survival
of the fittest, cute
bubble-butt spandex
sports bra out-
fit. CrossFit, burpee.
Protein, burps.
Physically unmoved by the
number of steps I need
to take per day
supplements, dietary restrictions
count a calorie
caloric-intake dates,
ingest my inhaler
each time my heart rate rises.
Sweat stains, armpits
don't like gray shirts.
De-odor…RANT
about my longevity
and my love life
like it's healthy
or something
that weighs a lot
on my shoulder press.

T-PAIN STARTED COVERING MY FAVORITE SONGS

T-Pain started covering my favorite songs and it got me feeling some type of way. And it sent chills up my spine, like I rediscovered I could feel something again. Like I was a belly-deep gospel singer in a past life with a ricochet voice that would reverberate off stained glass, sharply, staccato-like. They'd question the audacity of auto-tune to tweak such pure angelic voices with out-of-range star quality. I'd feel Gnarls Barkley *Crazy*, and we'd get so damn groovy with one another on the dance floor, but in a wholesome way, wicked later on. Like I was *country* and you were *soul* and we got drunk on *Tennessee Whiskey* and got whisked away into the jubilant chorus. Like it was a perpetual Saturday night, a *Black Ice* dancefloor, staring into your glow-in-the-dark irises. And, suddenly, we were *On Top of The Covers*, again. Always, always, having the time of our lives…never, never, ever thinking twice. *Does that make me Crazy? Does that make me Crazy?*

Maybe I am crazy
to think
you'd like that, too.

LANCEE WHETMAN

HI, MISS-DEMEANOR

He's a felon
Track record got him prison clout
He said: *hi, Miss-demeanor*
Now I can't wait for him to get out.

My felon landed behind bars
When he beat her with a hammer
But he's so hot in orange
Doing time in the slammer.

He's got nine more months
Got that lengthy criminal history
While he's there in handcuffs
I'll be his saving key.

What's a criminal without a felony?
I'll wait for him to get down on one knee
Three kids, a white picket fence
We'll move to a small town: him and me.

Have a thing for bad boys, I know
It's quite a horrible vice
But at least this love is requited
A thrilling and lawless paradise.

CHAPPED LIPS

WESTERN NIGHTS

free-ranging fringe
arid touch
spurs dig into
sheet scarcity
claws
on a cowboy

tumbleweed talks
the curvature of horseshoes
U, stake a claim.

ceremonial cactus
saguaro Joshua
deflowers the desert.

barebacked
into the night
they ride.

Yippee-ki-yay.

TRUE GRIT

we flashback to 1969. John Wayne,
fleeing history. old hickory
is well worn. western movies.

we saddle up on the couch,
Little Blackie leather
four white wooden legs.

I marshal you into my arms,
Texas Ranger wrangler, closer
to reprieve, are we,

into the indulgences
of the night,
like captured whiskey

in the throats of merriment.
my headstrong heart hangs
in your hands, suffering

to love. *is it adventure or antidote*
playing hostage with bed sheets?
I fall

into your snake
pit—
I am full.

CHAPPED LIPS

when I say *goodnight*, before
crossing the river to get back
home, over my shoulder

I peer around to you.
in the words of Charles Portis,
lookin' back is a bad habit.

LANCEE WHETMAN

INTERJECT

arrive after seven
improvise dinner
for hungered hearts
(and stomachs)
the roux and I
are saucy
whisked away
in whiskey's sure defeat
of the guardrail guardians
around my chest
listening to runaway stories
that brought us both to
convergence
brought us both to
emergence
and will soon bring us to
sheet *submergence*
altering each of our
Sundays to
come.
with tonight's
embraced departure,
we entertain the thought
of the electricity
we could have made
had our clothes
not interjected.

CHAPPED LIPS

GLOW IN THE DARK

body paint.
he insists on
a leg placement
on two calves, clutch
red-handed touch
and glow
muscle exposed
make art on me, *please*
in the low light
of the ultraviolet
writing Mandarin on my forearm
asking: where you at (WYA)
你在哪
answering: right here
under a *Blue Clear Sky.*
George Strait predictions
about how our bodily
thoroughfares
crisscross, comfortably.
we clash our hues
and heuristics
then wash the night off
down the drain.

LANCEE WHETMAN

POOL BOY

an undressed sundress
a summer pool
paper-thin tension
dive in deep
to feel wetness
on my skin
quench the day
in a way
I like
when water
and chlorine
interact
when clothes
are wayside
when a tanned
hand
skims
the surface—
I splash.

TUNDRA VIXEN

There's so much uncertainty with the changing of the seasons. Surely though, sunlight approaches kindlier on March mornings. *But will we look the same come summer?* For now, we spend time out-of-doors, tracking animals in the spring snow. There, a lynx. Then a moose. Here's a fox, female: You call me a *tundra vixen* with glints of golden orange. Strands aglow, as the sun rises up past horizontal. There is something on my mind, call it *spring fever*—airing out procreative urges, in the animal kingdom, that which we are a part of. You have the markings of a good father, whether or not you know it quite yet. What an honor would it be to obey our natural tendencies, to see our survival through another generation. As we step through the equinox portal, we are between living and dreaming. This landscape will never be the same the way that we remember it now, as codependent creatures. The future on our fur.

LANCEE WHETMAN

PUZZLE

I ask him to stop by
this cabin in my
secluded neck
of the woods
by the river. I have
fragments of myself
to share. I am ready to
be put together tonight
as I tell him:
There's   a

*   puzzle*
*   here*

*   in*
*   bedroom   my   that*
*   hasn't*

been
*   touched*

*   in*
*   months.*

LAGUNA ARSON

tips to grip, imprint where
we sleep as we study the bows
of bedsheet philosophy.

an inlet to an iris, this
pheromone sea, whiff.
wharf of extremities
extraneous to the heart—
harbingers of how-to-release.

the evaporation of tension
tidal pull, a part of this person
a plank of a leg, I walk
willingly, overboard
into the depths.
cloth, castaways of a closet
skin-scratched X
pillow-talk treasure
the rippling effect of a body.

call out, then capsize
my captain! when the
golden-hour sun is
landing, has landed, lands
here in this laguna
steam rolling off of the ocean
where W(h)etted water
meets arson.

LANCEE WHETMAN

CINDERELLA REIMAGINED

would that have saved them?
I don't know.
a clock
turned back into
midnight.
a pumpkin
let me patch up their heart.
fairy godmother,
I ask
if they can be the prince
instead of the princess
and still be
invited to the ball
with the rest of us
and dance
with
new pronouns
and without
glass slippers.

WOMAN IN S.T.E.M.

the convergence of chemicals // in our brains // gentle osmosis // as we learn how to fuse // *are we extraordinary phenomena?* // let the elements decide // remnants of stardust // an aftermath of an eager experiment // hypothetically hormonal // come combust // under fluorescence // we are nuclear // evolving into a bond // a solution // this symbiosis of blue recessives // helices for hands // transmit thermodynamic touch // just two living organisms // abiding by the laws of nature // XX and XY chromosomes // practicing biology

LANCEE WHETMAN

SNAP HIM NO FILTER

clock in and croissants
A.M. administration
click clack panic attacks
printer paper jams
mid-morning meltdowns
and anaphylactic shock
from a peanut butter M&M
epinephrine my coworker
clock out
calm me down
edible evening
waxing ~~croissant~~ crescent
starry
knight of wands
reversed
parmesan-truffle popcorn
and paranoia
THC
and a sea of blankets
recuperate from Monday
weakened by the weekend
snap him
no filter
guess we're
on that level now
I am on one
and now he's on me

CHAPPED LIPS

wet dream
pipe burst
baby, this is
too long
of a poem
and too long
of a life.

TO-DO LIST

- He makes a to-do list.
- I am on it.

OUTDATED DENNY'S

it's tradition.
we know
that he is supposed to pay
on the first date
at Denny's.
we are caffeinated up
when I learn
he switched to *they*
recently.
so now we're both confused
about norms
and how we
obey the conventions
of credit or cash payment
at the culmination of this hour.
pressing into my purse
and them, their wallet,
respectively.
we settle that
this remittance
must be shared equally—
we weren't quite fond
of omelets
(or conformity)
letting our buttery hands
melt against
the red-leather booth
spilling syrup

on our bill
even leaving a 20% tip
to our critical waiter
who stared us down
because we were
too smitten to care
for the dating conventions
greasing that
outdated Denny's.

CHAPPED LIPS

IF THE WORLD WAS ENDING

*would we be scared
or would it be surreal?*
putting reluctance
to the wayside
as the tide rises.
we revel in irrelevance—
a replay of two
torn apart
previously
by natural disasters
like shifting tectonics.
too-late telephone calls
tornado a path
as whispered breath
displaces skin and sea.
time is
an ingenious concept
in freefall—
we're predestined
to drown.
the earth
quakes, a lover's lower half.
*if the world was ending
would we?*

EARTHQUAKE

What is disaster? For me, it's finding fault in a faultless lover. The ground on which he walks neither quakes nor rumbles. Just his stomach when he forgets to eat. The frequency that we feel, in this moment, is calm. It's countenance and coming home. Or it was. If only seismometers measured doubt. Unsteady hands have to hold on, albeit too tightly sometimes. Confuse stability as an aftershock. Failure is geologic. Before the shatter. Before the motion of me trembles too far. Foundations don't rupture, they crack, when concrete caves in. Tempted, too much, by a tremor. Chart another lie like a data point; it only confirms that love destructs in me what I wish it would not. I am all rubble even when there's escape, lifelines. Choosing man over mantle, believing it's heroic or hedonistic. Intensity is a thrill. Shake under the stress of succumbing. Give in to shifty plates and persons. The velocity of a heart beat, I finally quell. Your name is a relinquishment of energy. At the epicenter of it all—me, letting go. Everything amplifies, then is eventually displaced.

LEAP YEAR

every four years
something out of the ordinary
happens on the 29th of February.
perhaps it's me
but today's bissextile
feels Byzantine.

I played,
Cold, Cold Heart
by Johnny Cash
while my car lubricated up
in -2 degrees Fahrenheit
headed off to work
like any "regular" day—
if a day can really
be classified as such.

ate my same meal-prepped lunch:
a recipe for normalcy
(or so I thought).

as my township's marriage commissioner,
I officiated a wedding
of two lovers
they hand-picked this date
so they would only have to
celebrate their anniversary
every four years
instead of one—
frugal
or fortunate?

that evening
my crush refereed
my basketball game
making subtle
hardwood jokes
as he called a foul
just so he could whistle at me.
underneath the net
as the opponent shot
free throws
he looked me in the eyes—
am I being literally
*court*ed?

after the win,
my teammate instructs
that the first three words
we should utter tomorrow
on March 1

must be *rabbit, rabbit, rabbit*
for good luck.
my Chinese zodiac: the Boar.
apparently,
(according to the internet,)
during this 365-day cycle
love is *not* in store for me—
the Hermit tarot card affirms
as I lock myself away in
single's sweet lair.

but I can't help but wonder,
four years from now,
what I'll be doing
with an extra day
and if you—
and the Year of the Rabbit—
will scamper on by
just like the rest.

DURATION UNKNOWN

Eyes have good drainage;
we want to change ourselves
so we watch the fireflies.

Statuary on the picnic blanket
the curious assertion
of a first kiss—
solstice is metamorphic.

July comes
almost as insistent.
Two lovers
veering further into summer.

Hieroglyphic initials
on willow bark
C&L
for ~~ever~~
duration unknown.

CONFECTIONARY CONCOC[K]TIONS

Confectionary concoc[k]tions
I've been tasting cotton-candy capriciousness.
Fi-zz-le
F   a   d   e

LANCEE WHETMAN

INSERTION

phalanges
number one, ok.
double digits
just enough.
trine no more—
too much.

CHAPPED LIPS

STOLEN LOVE

throw the dice
on an affair
mince a marriage
what's cooking?
trouble
and
tagliatelle
salt the water
spindles of noodles
canoodling
nudes.

nudibranchs
go down
deep.

WHAT'S BREWING?

Burnt coffee: a divine intervention. It could have just been bad luck, but I beg to differ. Finally, this tongue recognized displeasure for bittered beans, a metaphor for you, too. Acrid and harsh tones—I no longer salivate for caffeine and dopamine first thing in the morning. This a.m. kinesiology no longer shakes from your shade nor your stimulant—subtle tremors of the heart subside, as I opt for chamomile's calming effects. Getting over a dangerous reliance on something takes some getting used to. Pour over, French- ~~kissed~~ pressed, iced—in whatever form you ~~take~~ took. *Is there decorum in the drip? Revelry in the roast?* The smell of the caramelized cafe, where we met, is embedded with espresso. I don't know what's brewing within me now, but it's aromatic and aching. Today, I've got a new handle to hold, a different drink to down. Tea time, finally, without you in mind.

HOW ERGONOMIC ARE SOULMATES?

How many more days must I move through
alone?
Queuing up a ballad
of a scratched record tune
for another solo apartment dance sesh.
Interlace my left hand
with a maybe—
how ergonomic
are soulmates?
I may never know.
A measurement of audacity
I've got a malady
for unfinished puzzles
and begging
for the bare minimum.
Just another tale
of all-things unrequited:
Why do you always have to be
a dial away
from another *hello*
or another *goodbye*?

ELYSIAN END

mangle me // into an enigma // garble my words // like saltwater // spit me out to dry // sentence me to a rekindling // of us // *is there a worse fate?* // I am not sure // muster up some alliteration // again // aspire for an elysian end // this adherence // to false magic // has me on guard // or spellbound // impale myself on more self-doubt // floating in the moat of mixed signals // you're my tenet of disaster // furrow myself // into another fairytale // tell me // to stop listening // to rudimentary advice // from knights in shining armor // that we should just // try, try again

CHAPPED LIPS

CUMBERLAND GAP

what we are:
just each other's
muses. amuse me
abuse me
for the stories
we want others
to know
happened here
when our harangued
hearts
met
by happenstance
encumbered now
only by
the Cumberland

        G   A   P

LANCEE WHETMAN

PLEATED SKIRT

pleated skirt, the
audacity to be a woman.
belonging to this world
of unsolicited catcalls.
callous whistling
a chip-on-my-shoulder chirping
bluebird, blue jay, bluethroat
been   spreading
my
~~legs~~ wings.

SOUR(DOUGH)

You were wrong.
I was right.
How many times do we do this?
Fresh bread.
Kiss my forehead.
Kneading space.
Bonding gluten.
The timer beeps.
The dough has finished rising.
I am so sick of keeping score.
Score.
Score.

POLE DANCER

congeal mind and body
into vertical vocation.
do I yearn to separate the two
or am I courageous enough to
be desired?

in an on-and-off mode, I dial down
my existence. shrink a six-foot
figure to centimeters
stick-thin size
weightless woman.

on-sale sleep, dancing around
warning bells, tolling alarms
a heightened state of suspicion—
a normal night.

vegetative passion, eat my
greens—$1 fishnet bills.

tears muddle my reflection
thin-ply toilet paper to wipe
up my demise, stage of stilettos.

voice box drained
by inconsistencies
and inconsequential small talk.

CHAPPED LIPS

compliment my bravery to be here
longer than I need to—
rent-free skin.

temporality is a battery
I'm charging-station electric.
shock is underwhelming
graphic like graphite
double AA bust
energizing male egos
continuous usage.

pole promises
cleavage, a tease
cuddle immunity
cool belt cobalt
undo it
dance on a lap.

conflate wants with needs, but I still
know which one you are,
chasing morality after hours
in the church of the club.

there goes another twin flame,
blue for incongruities
sweat drips neon.

pick-me-up glitter,
count tips
from receding hairlines
hip-replacement wallets
degraded cents (sense).

strobe-light strip:
a career of constriction.

I will forever be
just an object
to you.

THE STREET I GREW UP ON AS MY PORN STAR NAME

Twelve Pines Drive.

Twelve for the number of dollar bills you'll fumble in my fishnets, fingering one-night-only lust.

Call it: *frugal desire.*

Pines for the tall stiletto pumps that root these legs to the stage. Poled thighs: you can't ground a girl defying gravity and G-strings. Quaking, pining for more.

Drive for driving you crazy. Drive you wild. Drive you to come back, come around again, like cul-de-sac

clickbait.

LITTLE MISS PISSED OFF

Done with fantasies and pre-ordained futures. Falling for strangers down Unicorn Lane who have no inclination to know my name. Gone are endorsements of duality. Discounting old ties—companionship is on clearance. Low is the lover's limbo stick. *How low can I go?* Pretty low apparently—must be my party trick.

Red-pen poems inking college-ruled notebooks with forceful bleed, hardly marginal. Old English letter-writing, cursive aspirations cloaked by Aspirin, antagonizing my beats per minute. My heart is handmade. *Where's the guy holding the glue gun?* Ammunition promises. Every *bang* followed by intangible hands. Silence felt with a thousand pinpricks—mistook it for a *spark*.

Playing poker with eventualities—the joker can only be laughed at so many times (you would think). *How comical is this chest-panging gnawing at my cleavage?* Mold me into model expectations. An eye-candy advertisement. Lacquer me in maybes. Perfume me in an afterthought. Quell my laughter with constant interrogation. Keep me for convenience. *Kum and Go* pit stop—transit to elsewhere. Gaslight a girl for fun. Road trip down a spine just for the sake of it.

Regret looks so regal on you; I please in pleasantries. *No more*, I say to the narcissist. Stop playing in my outskirts, opting in for quick access. So feral for forgiveness. Sew me up in excuses; eviscerate me by a text. A bouquet of strings and sutures from each re-opened door incision.

Solicitude is the next bachelorette. I'll tether myself to anything but relation to your name. This town was always yours for the taking, *but what if I were to make it mine out of spite?*

BAR NONE

whistle, whistle,
goes his dirty-talk lips
a cat call, he gives her
swish
of a hip.

a between-the-teeth:
hey hon'!
she distrusts lust
from the men
at Bar None.

closing time
that Saturday night,
he left an open tab of Cuervo,
she now sits
in front of the jury
replaying neon sorrow.

he gave her
a tequila shot
then throated hit.
her legs fought
his bedsheets
saying: *she wanted it*.

an antagonized bralette
braced for testimony.
she's fuming law
blood
and male acrimony.

sexual assault
in the first degree.
a now-prisoned man.
guilty!
(she won?)
what's done is done
but she still distrusts
the lust
from men
at Bar None.

SISYPHUS

calloused forget-me-nots
against the friction
of being here
with fear
of hitting the nail
right on the nose
nosy friends telling me
to burn the bridge
between us
now
twice cheated
I must
let dead dogs lie asleep
and roll boulders uphill
to make headstones
out of eternity.

SUNSET COFFEE SHOP

Sunset Coffee shop
overlooking suburban Sandy.
A mosaic of names etched
in the rickety wood tables
where we sat
and ingrained our L&M initials
for an unowned keepsake
to last
into the indefinite future.
We were Catholic school gossip
for a day
but no more than that
in chapel
where we held hands
under the Virgin Mary
until you parted
with the world
senior year.
I'd write about you
over Earl Grey
each Saturday at 7 a.m.
There, at that café,
I fell in love with poetry—
becoming my own Frankenstein
and giving life back
to your being
through my own
poetic creations.

KINGS OF HOMECOMING

pour my nickels
into a payphone.
momma said lettermans
are only first loves
and nothing more.
a wrong pair
of hearts fumbled
on the fifty-yard line—
I can feel it
stumblin'
stained green Achilles heels
as this small town unwinds
into the world.

havens cannot be made
in kings of homecoming
and Gatorade
will never quench
a queen.

LUDDITE LOVER

taking a romantic candlelit bath
to wash off all of my unsanitary
technological sexts
and *Tinder* transgressions.

the heart is under constant petrification:
evidence of generational unravel
pill-popping with hot water
thinning our blood
to be more sexually
fluid.

ceasing a cave-man upbringing—
let's wed our primal nature again.
something simple
something borrowed
something brute.

the number one
does not exist anymore—
poly
amorous mates
multifactored fates.

asking the nearest stop sign
if it wants to *go*
along for the
ride—
reverse cowgirl.

leave the waiting-for-them-to-change game
for someone else.

I'll come
over in the next century…

after I've finally recharged
my vibrator.

a Miss-
shapen Luddite
and
the science
of social-media matchmaking:
a series.

this persistent postage stamp
arrives at algorithm's door
for a booty call
knocking the heck out of a hashtag
#loveme
#LoveMe
#LOVEME!

CHAPPED LIPS

I WISH YOU WERE HERE

with me in our 60s Volkswagen van overlooking Santa Monica. The surfers catch waves. Onlookers toe their way though grain and leftover tide. I miss you in the way of knotted stomachs. It's a contradiction: us. To stand upright like it's drill. Going-through-the-motions healing. Remember the days of Monday karaoke? We'd duet: *I could drink a case of you.* Now, we're both sober so the song has lost much of its effect. *Cheers!* A toast to the only outlet: time. You're where the snow is, all studded tire track and fisherman's sweater—*the one I knitted for you?* I export this letter, jet-mail fast, high-priority postage. You're familiar with departing like wind. When you reply, I'll look up which time zone you are in, call you just in the nick of time—no more handwritten forgiveness.

THIRST

thirst
brought on
by Bordeaux wine
winks
& the intonation
of an *ohhhhhh*
reaching
for precipice.
negligees are obedient
in their unclasping.
a feat of female
entanglement:
hip supplication
bowing down
to every butterfly.
conclave licks
save me from drought.

BE GOOD, CHARLOTTE

in the 3x5
picture frame
smiles of our middle school selves.
you, laced with black-colored braces
over gapped teeth
in your emo era
pop punk and L.A. Colors hair gel
Green Day influences
us, front-row at a
Good Charlotte concert, our first date.
the authority of our youth:
bands whose lyrics we hardly knew.

in our second-period art class
you sketched a novice charcoal heart
and admitted you loved me
while also exclaiming a swear word:
shit!
landing you in the principal's office
and in the history books
at Crossroads Academy
as the *bad boy*.
my first report-card C
from us practicing early <u>Cardiology</u>.

photo booth film strip
tucked into my tattered copy of *Romeo and Juliet*
our adolescent kiss
captured in four clicks
holding acrylic hands until our
ceramic spring break (up).
your last words to me:
Be good, Charlotte. Be good.

strangers, come high school.
cocaine's stimulus, generational
self-prescription for pain.
sin and scar in your sinew now
lead in your margin doodles
gradients of red and bloodshot eyes
I do not recognize those irises
the irony of who we become.
is it too late for good
music and good influences?
we were The Young and The Hopeless.

saving these tears when
I see our young selves
sculptured in graduation regalia
a snapshot of the Class of 2013
they called your name.
switch the tassel
switch your behavior, I pray
you get into the local art institute.

CHAPPED LIPS

how confusing it can be:
color theory, years later.
violet is just a different name
for purple.
she's surrounded by bruises
you are the investigation's first suspect
since you were there
that night, they say,
when she died:
The Chronicles of Life and Death.

and I don't remember how
to frame you in light's best value
to preserve your purest hues
knowing what I know
or just what people think
of your darkness.

and I don't know which border
you belong in anymore:
nothing is ever truly black-and-white.

but I do remember we were once complementary
and I do remember listening to Good Charlotte.

A New Beginning, I hope you draw that, for yourself.

WHISTLEBLOWER VOICE

acetone and lacquered cuticle
bathroom fumigation
perfume radiation
Daisy by Marc Jacobs.

do I reek of flowery innocence?

age-gapped, us
me, a barely licensed juvenile
you, barely a silver fox.

a three-story condominium
downtown, working
for the "man."
how governmental.

this top-secret affair
tells me to *hush*.
let's have a sleepover.
have you ever laid in
a king-sized bed before?

I'll do anything once
at that age, guided by
the YOLO doctrine.

CHAPPED LIPS

I learn two things:
that his niece
is a year younger
than I am in high school
and that there is something
called #MeToo.

MAYONNAISE

Play something Lo-Fi or something with an acoustic guitar. Light the incense, light the candle. Pivot towards sriracha sauce for every failed homemade mayonnaise attempt. Butcher the fries (but in the best way). 500-degree crisp. Cornstarch observations. What's the next step? The carbs are what we melt for, what we break diets for—but not dinner plans. I guess relationships are like recipes—a little bit of this and that. Thickening. Thinning. Heating. Cooling. How are you? How would you like your tea? Pull up a chair. My dear, let tonight be sustenance.

MIGHTY CONVINCING

a straitjacket of
aggrandized daydreams.

watching a wish
go up in smoke.

split in two
halves of a Gemini.

*abracada-
bra*! is off.

casting levitating stars
and swaggered cottontails
back into a black hat.

daggered by the ace of spades.

a hot-flash touch
an outburst of doves
just-vanishing friend zones.

I could use some
mighty convincing that
I am pure magic and
this isn't just
an invisible
trick.

RED HERRING

His red-herring hands
knock.
He's always in a
heightened state of
sorry pouring out
from each late-night call.
It's an allowance of
unlocked doors
to be held by
half hazard
half man.
Tonight
charisma's gentle persuasion
coaxes each fragile vulnerability
into submission
especially when
there's empty real estate
by this right ~~wrong~~ side
he's willing to occupy.

A pulse deluge—
trance or
nightmare?
There is no trace
of him come morning
except
an unlocked door.

CHAPPED LIPS

ANTIDOTE

Your poison:
so easy to take
with a shot-up smile.

Chasing coursing recurrences
with high hopes
that what you do
to my bloodstream
burns.

In surrender
to needle
on my knees
dear
push it down
again
as I subsume into oxy.

Trusting that you'll
tailrace these tears
away—
this addict's rationale
is to ingest finality.

It's time I choose control
greet unknown
with long-sleeved arms
to hide the decision
to become brave enough.

LANCEE WHETMAN

Stepping into the
light stings, at first.
The leaving antidote,
I find,
burns you, too.

NOTHING PERSONAL, JUST NEVER WANT TO SEE YOU AGAIN

Left off as a lover
got framed as a friend
acted like an acquaintance
was stood up like a stranger.

How ubiquitous is convenience?
Choosing what fragments of me
to string along this city.

Without warning
weighted down by breadcrumbs
back-to-back shocks to my
nervous system—
confusing it with nirvana.

Drawing back my eyes
into introversion.
An internal cry
as you cusp her hand
but can never seem to unearth
her name around me.

At the next unexpected run-in
you say: *I've been reading your poetry.*
Tell me how to define confusion.

Perhaps the problem here is
that we won't admit
that we both
still care
but know that we
shouldn't.

COMING-DOWN COMEUPPANCE

The comedown comes after the *come over* text. Butterflies in your belly, from the booty-call correspondence. The comedown comes after you realize you were just a body, to him. He liked your bodice over your brains, as he brandished his marijuana tongue at 2 a.m.—the time of temptation and telling you sweet nothings. The comedown comes after he came first, then left you there on the left side of the bed (all while stealing the comforter—how discomforting). He didn't cuddle you or contemplate your feelings. The comedown comes when you clean the globs of mascara that dripped down your face like blackened watercolor. When he didn't call back the next day…or the next…or the weeks thereafter. The comedown comes when you realize he just used you for his own selfish high.

Come down to earth, darling.
Hit rock bottom
before giving him
his coming-down
comeuppance.

JEST

spade-digging
with the sutras—
girthy enlightenment.

have I reached a higher
plane of existence
or am I just evaporating
into niceties?

this heart is harlequin-ed out
joke's over.

queen of diamonds—
a card-deck conspiracy.

ring-encircled jest.
laugh about forever
like it's a joke.
poke fun
at being in love
with me.

PYROTECHNICS

teach me about pyrotechnics
and probabilities.

ignite flares
that flicker
then wane—
waiting for
a glimmer of hope,
for that
spark
to fire
for you
again.

I'VE SEEN IT ALL BEFORE

It's strange how I count sunrises like I'll ever be able to keep track. The way fingertips balance a basketball in finite orbit. The way his eyes linger on the cheeky young blonde. The way a strand of hair splits at its end. What we notice in the most micro form, I have found, is often the most important. You know, the way Amos Lee's song, *Seen It All Before*, plays like premonition. The way I draw the Tower tarot card five days in a row—the magic is exacting. Sudden change, upheaval, chaos, revelation, awakening. It's strange, you know, how ego can estrange us, entangle us. Like life is a tradeoff between what we are able to withstand and what we want. Like a deep-seeded pang burning in your chest after a hard workout. Like how you skip rocks knowing they ultimately sink, never to resurface again. It's strange, ain't it? Like the way your gut hesitates when a lover says, *she's just a friend*.

RIGHT-OF-WAY

I've got the write-of-way, right?

there's a tough girl somewhere
behind this sad poem
I just know it.

you, tuck a tuft of hair
behind my ear
touch my inner thigh
read me *King Lear*
and sear me
by the season's end.
scarred by autumn
scared of spring
twining our hands
emulating the movies.

when will I be unaffected by time?

I'm late on my way
to the unravel
making sense of
mystification
misted eyes

                                                and missing you.

LANCEE WHETMAN

TIL' DEATH (OR DIVORCE) DO US PART

an open bar of apathy.
my plus one:
an eon of loneliness.
cud chewing
on chrysanthemums
and congratulations.

misanthropic meat eater:
my dinner-platter selection.
I witness stardust elopers
elongating their jaws
to unionize.

indifferent to forever
I puke in the last pew
to avoid the High Priestess.

light bleeds
through stained-glass interstices.
a rainbow
at marriage's pre-funeral—
the graveyard is quickly graying.
last names are seasonal
soon-to-be laid to rest
in their respective tombstones.
dial the mortician to ask
the going rate

CHAPPED LIPS

for a couple's coffin.

she takes the orthodox route,
adopting his rusted silver.

decaying bouquets,
I catch.

the best man
dips my shrimp
cocktail dress
on ice.
I know I'm cold—
I'll last longer that way.

a morsel
of a moan appetizer
corrupted from his throat.
belt-buckle hickey.
buttoning up our composure.

road trip
back to the ceremony
on stiletto. point
out the cliche vows
toast to my kidneys
ask the almighty speakers
for one last slow dance.

bride-groom fashion-ably
late to the underworld.

Til' death
(or divorce)
do us part…
they recite
in front of us all.

007

The bonds we keep are peerless
when you woo a womanizer. It's a crime

to deprive a person of agency.
Choices. Chase a thrill. Double oh

several other women
in holster holds—chest-strapped closeness.

It's operative to sleuth.
To him, I am Lancee Drew

just another inquisitively fictitious
girl. Give me gut-check intuition—

it's a six-sense state.
The incongruence of an answer:

cataclysmic.

That's part one of the series—
the mysterious affair.

Make me mad.
Make me magnum.

MAKING UP

Performance is cerebral. Vex
a cortex and say you're a brainiac

babe. Halve my bed and make it part
forgiveness. Silence her name.

Scream mine out. Springs
are relapse. I give alms

to your skin pensando que
es tu alma.

CHAPPED LIPS

STINGING NETTLE

I covet breath more than anything these days. Coat my lungs with mountain air and fog-clearing promises to myself to be mesmerized more often. When the exhale evaporates, so do you, into the thinness of oxygen. Each inclined step I take, my pulse beats from something other than your poison-ivy touch—a rash decision at an irrational time. I am fond of Gaia—no longer the guy. *How handsome are these heights?* My waterproof boots trudge, in a good way, like I earned the elevation. Gaining a view but not losing my hard-earned grounding. Earthen connection. Muddy steps, more careful now, to avoid the stinging nettle. Comforted by the camouflage of foliage and falling leaves, decay is okay. Going down no longer feels like a *TIMBER!* but more like a tender trek. It's the time of fresh starts, leaving a serene script with every soled imprint. An inalienable lightness, a long-awaited laugh. I watch the wildflowers, wilting now, wanting to change.

FRICTION

four chords and
several years ago
it was February.
we stayed inside and
forgot about the rules
of engagement.
bowed out of a promise.
fumbled a heart.
it was not the appropriate
time for a breakdown,
beside you,
but it happened.

there goes another
crumpled ~~love~~ poem
crumpled sheet
crumpled heart.

be it sentimental pessimism
as we unparalleled our paths.
perpetually perpendicular,
right-angle our intentions
out of rigid expectations
until our geometry
eventually turns
to *friction*.

CHAPPED LIPS

PILOTS

The worst thing you
can ever tell
a grown man with wings
is:
*you're
grounded.*

BEEN BITTEN BEFORE

Thump-eyed and thunderstruck
I've weathered one too many of his
short-tempered storms.
Bruise-smacked and a custom-built collapse
standing guarded, gripping a payphone—
calls to sanctuary from domestic disturbance.
Reaching for a familial furry-friend comfort
I outstretch my harrowed hand
but am greeted with snarled aggression.
The owner reassures me:
Oh, don't worry, he won't hurt you
and I wonder where I've heard that familiar lie before.

CHAPPED LIPS

TINY ENCOUNTERS WITH RESTRAINT

I skip that static George Strait song
that once blasted through
your 1980 Ford Bronco
barreling out of Earl's Diner gravel
to get us home to
make something grand of ourselves
in this small town
but what we made
that day
was life
but we did not know it
when we said
our hundredth
goodbye—
ironically on
Centennial St.

Met with my
physician today
and a test is positive
but I am not.
I bite my
minor-detail tongue.
I do not dare
tell you
the child is yours.

DON'T FORGET ME

I've stolen myself back
from every prospective
left-fingered lover
promising a veil.
Maybe marriage
gives me goosebumps—
lace, tulle, organza gowns
and runny mascara
as I ride shotgun with cold feet
our just-*not*-married cans
clinking the asphalt.
Dodged him with
don't forget me static:
that one missed forever
still misses
me.

SPLINTER

There's an entry fee for love. Chainsmoke the atmosphere. Break Cupid's arrow as catharsis. I won't listen to my therapist, but I will listen to any advice given by Denzel Washington: *Give no guy a second chance.* I've got keyed-car rage mixed with doe-eyed sadness. A lie so claustrophobic. I want cupped hands as a begging vessel. Vacillate on who is the suspect. Make me that girl in the he-is-checking-out-other-women meme. Call it a blind spot. Let the LAX airport be my breaking point. When splintered trust pierces skin, it's fatal at its finest.

WOMEN MY AGE ARE...

doing at-home laser hair removal treatments with protective eyewear listening to the latest episode of *Crime Junkie* while ZAP ZAP ZAPPING away at each cubby-holed pore // group-chatting the girl gang during work hours to plan the next book-club selection // dumping their reality TV Chad boyfriends whose outdated life mantra is "gym, tan, laundry" // still single, researching egg-freezing and in-vitro fertilization because they'd rather be artificially inseminated in their mid-thirties than be bound to any of the buffoons in the dating pool // supporting themselves financially, emotionally, and in all the -lly ways // adopting a litter of sled dogs // putting down roots and down payments, first-home buyers and ballin' on a budget—the economy waits for no (wo)man // getting bailed out or bailing someone out // van-lifing it in some obscure Pacific Northwest forest or watching a Planet Earth documentary on their IKEA cross-sectional on a Friday night // either too hot or too cold // like the old adage, going to college to get more knowlledggeeee.

PRETTY LIKE POETRY

anything is a poem
if you flirt with it
enough
or format it
to look pretty.

do you like me **BOLD** or *italicized?*

AT THE CLUB

I want you with disco urgency. Worst-behavior philosophy. EDM's automatic salvation. Come claim these wallflower hips. So demure to sheer skin in a wink's time; qualify the expression as sex hemisphere. Ode-ing evocative poems. Flavor launch a tongue. How do I encourage buttons to fall completely off?

HOLDING TOO TIGHTLY

Unreasonable demands.
Contingent-ship.
Control is ultimatum.
Could we clutch and call it *cheeky*?
Could we constrict and call it *cuddling*?
Restrict each other to eternity?

LIMBO

What we are is always inconclusive. Bide me some permanence. Whisper to me all the coincidences in this lifetime. Minimize what our cells want to conduct. Counteract a touch then leave me stranded in *maybes*. The percentage of honesty that I request is just theorem. Far surpassed the age where hope is a character I vouch for. Each poem, merely a diary entry, enters and never leaves—unlike you. Every *please* is more desperate than the last. It's a loon with a lunatic watching: park-bench loneliness. The only confessional here is the bar, and I have nothing left to tip. Undo a belt just to be more insecure about revealing myself to ceilings. Make a Motel 6 out of me—transience my only vanguard.

CHAPPED LIPS

THIS POEM HAS ALREADY BEEN WRITTEN, BUT...

I am still listening
to "Before He Cheats"
by Carrie Underwood.

He is still
Snapchatting women
who do not know my name.

I still
ride the bicycle-of-grief stages
to work.

I am in a still photo
at every small-town
grocery-store run in.

I was still
as he touched himself.

Still confused
when he said
he was turned on
but did not tell me
that she was the reason
why.

EXILE

I say: *Come over*
to be upholstered to the bed frame
so that we may mold into something dual.
*What permanency do we need
other than the night?*
Devour my mind
ricochet off my lips
we're both ever-expanding here.
Morning closes in quick
goodbye becomes
more and more dilatory.
Lock-jawed with staying.
Your leaving: cruel punishment.
We exile each other's eyes
and as you drive away
we slowly start to become
more and more
out of focus.

CHAPPED LIPS

BOY WITH THE BLUES

Dripping in verses not yet constructed
I'm beguiled in his blues sanctuary.
Rhythm tandem with these emotional ties
ears attuned to moaning bass
reverberating electric tongue tips
and thread counts
guitar-infused
sound supplier
break the strings
hair-strand
strum my brunette breathless.
His voice,
whiskey octave-dropped
inflections
another hit of the high note—
cymbals clash (and so do we).
Resonance in wavelength-ed hair.
Reprise.
Reprise.
Reprise.
In the comedown of the chorus
conducting this duvet duet in measures:
Hold for four.
For two.
For one.
Half a second.
One-eighth.
Until conclusion.

ABOUT THE AUTHOR

Lancee Whetman's "ChapStick" of choice: Moon Valley Organics Velvety Vanilla Beeswax Lip Balm. She likes afternoon naps; huckleberry kombucha; a wardrobe of flowy flowery dresses; the music of John Prine, Bob Dylan, and Stevie Nicks; and the scent of spruce trees. She hates mixed signals, lip service, dating in this era, and of course, chapped lips.

ACKNOWLEDGMENTS

My gratitude goes out to the upstanding Zachary Olson, Emily Lane Schlick, and Claire Prasad for beta reading, proofing, and line editing this chapped collection. To Skyler Karajanis, for designing the just-kissed cover art. To Kristina Konstantinova, for formatting the heart of this paginal collection. And to love, for its obligatory lessons and for making me fall, like a fool, one too many times.